BTS
K-POP KINGS

Carolyn McHugh

sona
BOOKS

First published in the UK 2026 by Sona Books an imprint of Danann Media Publishing Ltd.
Original material Copyright © 2021 Danann Publishing Ltd.

CAT NO: SON0727

Photography courtesy of

Getty images:

- Jeff Kravitz/FilmMagic
- Chris Polk
- The Chosunilbo JNS/Imazins
- THE FACT/Imazins
- JTBC PLUS/Imazins
- Han Myung-Gu/WireImage
- ilgan Sports/Multi-Bits
- Kevin Winter
- Big Hit Entertainment/AMA2020
- YOAN VALAT/AFP
- Rich Fury
- Kevin Winter/AMA2017
- Kevin Mazur/WireImage
- Chelsea Guglielmino
- Chris Polk/AMA2017
- C Flanigan
- ROBYN BECK/AFP
- The Chosunilbo JNS/Imazins
- THE FACT/Imazins
- YOAN VALAT/AFP

Yonhap/Newcom/Alamy Live News
Other images Wiki Commons

Book layout & design Darren Grice at Ctrl-d
Editor Tom O'Neill

Made in EU
ISBN: 978-1-917259-84-2

CONTENTS

01 MEET BTS

For the first time since the birth of rock and roll in the USA more than 60 years ago, Western pop music's world domination has been challenged. Leading the charge are the seven shining South Korean stars who form the K-pop phenomenon BTS – the highest grossing boy band in the world.

In just over a decade, the BTS boys - RM, Suga, J-Hope, Jin, Jimin, V and Jungkook - have built on their success in their South Korean homeland to become a truly global phenomenon. They have sold an estimated 60-70 million physical albums worldwide, an achievement that puts them among the best-selling artists of the modern era. However, in today's streaming-driven industry, their reach is better captured by album-equivalent sales - a metric that combines physical and digital album purchases with streaming activity. By 2026, BTS surpassed 500 million album-equivalent units globally, making them the best-selling Asian act in history and one of the biggest music acts worldwide.

With their dominance extending across every major platform, BTS has topped the iTunes charts in more than 100 countries and amassed tens of billions of streams, making them one of the most-streamed groups in the history of Spotify.

In the United States, they became the first South Korean group to perform at the Grammys and also to be nominated for a Grammy Award, earning five nominations between 2021 and 2023.

Between 2022 and 2025, BTS achieved something unprecedented: they remained the world's biggest group even while taking a hiatus to fulfil their mandatory South Korean military service. All seven members completed their duty during those years, while also using the time to release successful solo albums and prove themselves as individual artists.

In January 2026, with all seven members reunited following their mandatory military service, BTS are back with their new album ARIRANG and a historic world tour across five continents, spanning more than 85 dates.

AFTER NEARLY FOUR YEARS APART, THE BIGGEST BOY BAND IN THE WORLD IS BACK.

BTS bow at the end of their concert at Gwanghwamun Square in Seoul on March 21, 2026

FROM BULLETPROOF BOY SCOUTS TO BEYOND THE SCENE

The name BTS comes from the Korean word Bangtan Sonyeondan, which translates as 'Bulletproof Boy Scouts'. The BTS boys chose this to exemplify their aim of 'blocking out stereotypes, criticisms and expectations' which can rain down on teenagers and young adults 'like bullets'.

Many of their self-penned songs follow this theme -- helping young people to withstand the pressures and problems of modern society which can impact on their mental health.

Since July 2017, BTS has said that their name now also stands for 'Beyond The Scene' to reflect the fact that their fans are moving forward by overcoming the realities they face.

But don't be fooled into thinking that their music is therefore mournful and introspective. Quite the reverse. The boys want their sound to lift people up and give them energy and self-confidence - think rap, hip hop, pop and EDM (electric dance music). Now add some of the slickest, tightest, most elaborate choreography around. One look at a BTS video will show you why they have become a global force to be reckoned with.

BTS stand out from the K-pop crowd by writing their own material which has socially conscious lyricss, creating and managing most of their own social media, focussing on albums rather than singles, and talking openly to fans about their own personal struggles in life. This all combines to give them an incredible allure which has accelerated their ascendency into Western mainstream music.

BTS perform 'DNA' onstage during the 2017 American Music Awards at Microsoft Theater on November 19, 2017 in Los Angeles

TIME

2012
Opened a Twitter account to kick off communication with their fans

2013
First hit single 'No More Dream'

2014
Skool Luv Affair album makes No 3 on US Billboard chart

2015
I Need U gives BTS its first music show win SBS MTV's 'The Show' since their debut performance

2016
Achieve first Album of the Year at Melon Music Awards with Young Forever

2017
BTS become first South Korean band to win a Billboard music award, beating acts such as Justin Bieber and Selena Gomez to become 'Top Social Artist'

2018
BTS enjoy their first No I on the US Billboard 200 chart with Love Yourself the first ever K-pop album to top the American chart Launch 'Love Myself'' campaign with UNICEF to end violence against children

2019

Make first appearance at the US Grammy Awards show when they present artist H.E.R with the prize for Best R&B album

2020

Smash hit Dynamite the band's first single sung in the English language shoots to No I on the US Billboard Hot 100 chart and reaches Number I in the UK

BTS is nominated for its first Grammy Award for 'Pop Duo/Group performance'

2022

The anthology album Proof was released as BTS's final group album before the band announced a hiatus for mandatory military service and solo activities. Jin first to enlist (Dec 13, 2022), whilst RM released Indigo

2023

Jimin's hit single Like Crazy from his solo album Face reached I on Billboard Hot 100), Suga released D-Day album + a world tour, V released Layover album and Jungkook's Seven becomes massive global hit.

By December, RM, Jimin, V, and Jungkook are all enlisted

2024

J-Hope releases Hope on the Street Vol. I album + a docuseries, RM's Right Place, Wrong Person album, Jimin's MUSE album and Jin's Happy album.

Jin was the first member discharged from military service, followed by J-Hope

2025

Jin's Echo album is released, and all members reunited in studio, rehearsing for comeback.

2026

World tour announced. New group album release. Tours begin in South Korea. They are back.

62 THE BOYS

Meet the seven superstars of BTS. The talented septet who live and work together, co-writing and producing much of their music. They describe themselves as 'friends, business partners and roommates'.

RM

LEADER & RAPPER

RM is the leader of the boys – the whole band was essentially built around him – and, because he has the most fluent English, he's the one who usually acts as the main spokesman in interviews and personal appearances.

Born Kim Nam-jun in South Korea on 12 September 1994, RM grew up with his younger sister in the Ilsan-gu area which is less than 20 miles from the capital Seoul.

Top US sitcom Friends is responsible for RM's great English language skills. His mother bought him the complete box set and he watched all 10 series, first with South Korean subtitles, then with English subtitles and then with no subtitles at all.

RM's interest in hip hop and rap began when he was aged 11, then, as a teenager, he began rapping in local amateur hip hop circles. Using the name Runch Randa, RM became increasingly active in the underground Korean hip hop scene and eventually came to the attention of Big Hit CEO Bang Si-hyuk who invited him to join his Big Hit Entertainment studio as an idol trainee in 2010. Working with his producer Pdogg, Bang had the idea of building a hip hop group around RM and this eventually became idol group BTS.

During his time at the studio RM used the stage name Rap Monster which had been coined by fans. But he now prefers the abbreviation 'RM'.

Now RM produces and writes lyrics for many tracks on all BTS albums.

When BTS announced their hiatus in 2022 to fulfil mandatory military service, RM seized the opportunity to explore his artistic vision beyond the group.

His first official solo album, Indigo, was released just weeks before his military enlistment. Described as an "archive of RM's twenties," the album was a deeply personal exploration of art, identity, and introspection.

RM drew inspiration from visual art – he's an enthusiastic art collector – and the album felt like walking through a gallery of his experiences. Standout tracks included Wild Flower featuring Youjeen, which topped Korean charts, and Still Life, a reflective piece about finding peace amid chaos.

Indigo debuted at #3 on the Billboard 200 and topped iTunes charts in 67 countries.

In an extraordinary move, RM released his second solo album, Right Place, Wrong Person, while serving in the military. The album had been completed before enlistment and was released in May 2024. This 11-track project took an even more experimental turn than Indigo, exploring themes of identity and belonging. Lead single LOST! featured a striking music video showcasing RM's willingness to take creative risk. Other standout tracks included Nuts, Domodachi, and Around the World in a Day.

The album debuted in the top 5 on the Billboard 200, a remarkable achievement for an artist on military hiatus. And still during his military service period, RM's previously recorded collaborations continued to be released:

- Neva Play with Megan Thee Stallion (September 2024)
- Don't Cry featured on Fall Out Boy's So Much (For) Stardust album (2023)
- Over the Rainbow with Anderson .Paak
- Contributions to Lil Nas X projects

SUGA

LEAD RAPPER

Suga is the stage name of Min Yun-ki, one of the band's lead rappers. The name Suga is said to come from the first syllables of the words 'shooting guard' which was the position he played in basketball as a student. However, many fans say it is because he is sweet as sugar.

He was born on 9 March 1993 in Daegu, South Korea, the younger of two sons. He developed his interest in hip hop and rap and began to write his own material when he was around 13 years old. By the time he was 17 he had got a part-time job at a record studio and began doing more composing and arranging music.

Much like RM, Suga was already a popular underground rapper when he first signed with Big Hit as a music producer. As well as making a name for himself as an underground rapper known as 'Gloss', he was part of the hip hop crew D-Town.

He trained under Big Hit Entertainment alongside RM and J-Hope for three years before making his debut.

He has produced and written lyrics for a variety of tracks on all of BTS' albums. The Korea Music Copyright Association credits him with more than 70 registered songs.

As well as his stage name of Suga, he also uses the alias Agust D, which is derived from the initials DT, short for his home Daegu Town, mixed with the word 'Suga' spelled backwards. For example when he released his self-titled mixtape in 2016 it was credited to Agust D.

As one of the oldest members of BTS, he is something of a father-figure to the younger members of the band.

During BTS's hiatus, Suga stepped fully into the spotlight with the release of his first official solo studio album, D-DAY, in April 2023. Released under his Agust D persona, the album served as the powerful final chapter of a trilogy that began with Agust D (2016) and D-2 (2020).

Where the earlier projects captured anger, ambition, and survival, D-DAY felt reflective and resolute - an album about confronting the past and choosing how to move forward.

The project featured standout collaborations that fans immediately embraced. People Pt. 2 with IU revisited themes of emotional distance and connection, while Haegeum blended traditional Korean instrumentation with sharp social commentary.

Tracks like Snooze, featuring the late Ryuichi Sakamoto and Woosung of The Rose, showcased Suga's maturity as both a producer and storyteller, offering comfort to younger artists navigating pressure and burnout.

Following the album's release, Suga embarked on the Agust D D-DAY Tour, becoming the first BTS member to hold a full-scale solo world tour.

J-HOPE

MAIN DANCER, RAPPER, SUB-VOCALIST

J-Hope is the stage name of Jung Ho-seok, the group's main dancer/choreographer and an accomplished rapper.

J-Hope was born in Gwangju, south-west South Korea, where he lived with his parents and elder sister. Before signing with Big Hit Entertainment as a trainee idol when he was 15, he had taken dance classes for six years, winning various local and national prizes and becoming part of the underground dance team Neuron. J-Hope's dance style is influenced by street and freestyle hip hop dance - he's upbeat and energetic, with precise poppin' and lockin' moves. BTS are acknowledged as having some of the most complicated choreography in K-pop.

J-Hope unveiled a bold new side of himself as a solo artist in 2022, beginning with the release of his first official solo studio album, Jack In The Box, in July. Departing from his bright, upbeat image, the album introduced a darker, more introspective sound rooted in old-school hip-hop.

Through tracks like MORE and Arson, J-Hope explored themes of ambition, pressure, identity, and the cost of success, signalling a clear artistic turning point.

Later that month, J-Hope made history as the first Korean artist to headline the US festival Lollapalooza, delivering a commanding set that firmly established him as a global solo performer.

In 2023, he followed up with the heartfelt single 'on the street,' a collaboration with J. Cole that reflected on gratitude, growth, and his journey as an artist. The track was released just days before his enlistment, making it an emotional farewell to fans.

J-Hope began his mandatory military service in April 2023, and even while enlisted his creative presence remained strong. In March 2024, he released Hope on the Street Vol. 1, a dance-focused solo project accompanied by a documentary series celebrating his roots as a street dancer.

JIN

VOCALIST & VISUAL

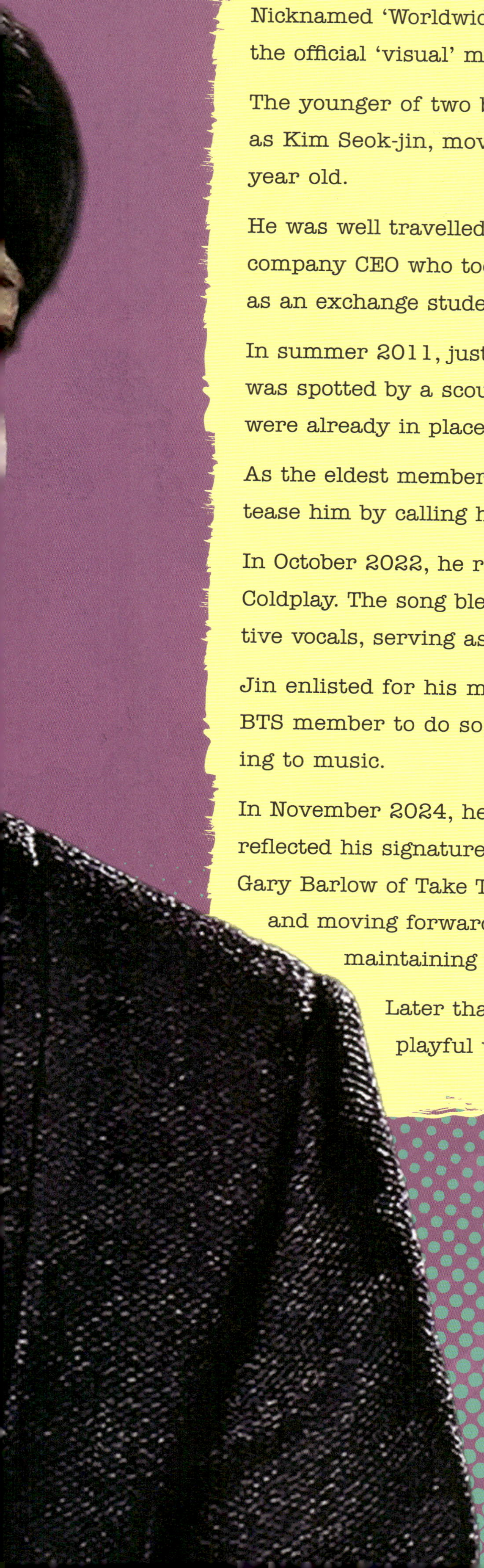

Nicknamed 'Worldwide Handsome', (WWH for short), Jin is the eldest boy in the group and the official 'visual' member.

The younger of two brothers, he was born on 4 December 1992 in Anyang, Gyeonggi-do, as Kim Seok-jin, moving to Gwacheon, near the capital city of Seoul, when he was just a year old.

He was well travelled even before hitting the road as a pop star because his father was a company CEO who took Jin with him on business trips. Jin also spent a year in Australia as an exchange student during his middle school years.

In summer 2011, just three months after joining Konkuk University to study acting, Jin was spotted by a scout from Big Hit and joined BTS, alongside RM, Suga and J-Hope who were already in place.

As the eldest member of BTS Jin is happy to act as a mentor to the other members, who tease him by calling him 'omma', which means 'mum' in South Korean.

In October 2022, he released The Astronaut, his first official solo single, co-written with Coldplay. The song blended Brit-pop and soft rock influences with Jin's unmistakably emotive vocals, serving as a heartfelt farewell to fans ahead of his enlistment.

Jin enlisted for his mandatory military service in December 2022, becoming the first BTS member to do so, and following his discharge in June 2024 wasted no time returning to music.

In November 2024, he released his first solo EP, Happy, a bright and uplifting project that reflected his signature optimism. Led by the energetic single Running Wild, produced by Gary Barlow of Take That, the EP leaned into pop-rock sounds and themes of joy, resilience, and moving forward. Tracks like I'll Be There showcased Jin's emotional range, while maintaining the warmth fans associate so strongly with him.

Later that year, Jin delighted fans by officially revisiting Super Tuna, the playful viral hit that had become an unexpected fan favourite.

JIMIN

LEAD DANCER & VOCALIST

Dance king Jimin is known for his work ethic and competitive side and describes himself as a perfectionist.

He was born Park Ji-Min, in Geumjeong, Busan, on the south-east coast of South Korea where he lived with his parents and younger brother.

Before joining Big Hit he had studied contemporary and modern dance and did so well that teachers suggested he audition for an idol studio, which he did successfully with Big Hit in 2012.

Jimin stepped into his solo spotlight with the same passion and artistry that fans had admired for years - but with a whole new level of personal expression. In March 2023, he released his first full solo album, FACE, a milestone that showcased his growth as both a singer and performer.

The album's standout tracks, like Like Crazy and Vibe, explored themes of self-reflection, love, and finding one's place in the world, striking a deep chord with fans everywhere. From soaring vocals to emotionally charged performances, Jimin poured everything into every note.

FACE didn't just win hearts - it topped South Korea's Gaon Album Chart at #1 and made waves internationally. He completed his 18 months of military service between December 2023 and June 2025.

V
VOCALIST & VISUAL

V was born Kim Tae-hyung, in Daegu, South Korea and grew up, with his younger brother and sister, in Geochang County. He says that his stage name V stands for the word 'victory'.

He took singing and saxophone lessons as a child and became a trainee idol with Big Hit Entertainment in 2011 aged 17. He is highly praised for his 'deep and husky' singing voice but has also worked hard enough to make the dance line within the band.

In 2016, V made his acting debut with a supporting role in the South Korean television historical drama 'Hwarang: The Poet Warrior Youth'.

In December 2022, V dropped his first solo studio album, Layover, giving fans a full taste of his rich baritone, experimental vibes, and genre-blending creativity. From smooth R&B to jazzy touches and moody pop, the album showed off just how fearless he is when it comes to trying new sounds.

Layover was a huge hit, debuting at #2 on the Billboard 200 and topping charts in South Korea and around the world. Singles like Love Me Again and Rainy Days quickly became fan favourites, with ARMY praising V's immersive storytelling.

Alongside the album, V treated fans to live performances and intimate fan events that were equal parts stunning and heartwarming - think breathtaking vocals, playful stage moments, and that magnetic energy he can bring.

JUNGK

VOCALIST, DANCER & SUB-RAPPER

Jungkook is the youngest member of the group, having been born Jeon Jung-kook in 1997 in Busan on South Korea's southeast coast, where he lived with his parents and elder brother.

He decided he wanted to be a singer when he was 14 and auditioned for the South Korean talent show Superstar K in 2011. Although he didn't win the contest, the exposure got him noticed and he went on to receive offers from seven big K-pop studios. But he turned them all down in favour of joining the idol training programme at Big Hit Entertainment, and BTS, reportedly because he was a such a big fan of RM.

Jungkook embraced his evolution as a solo artist during BTS's hiatus era, and in July 2023 released his first full solo project, Golden. He experimented with new sounds while staying true to his emotive style, particularly in Stay Alive and Euphoria Pt. 2 where he explored themes of self-discovery, perseverance, and the pressures of fame.

Golden achieved remarkable commercial success, topping the Billboard 200, as well as charts in South Korea, Japan, and multiple international markets.

Accompanying the release, Jungkook embarked on a limited world tour, combining dynamic performances with fun fan interactions, and sneak peeks of unreleased songs.

OOK

03

TEAMWORK MAKES THE DREAM WORK

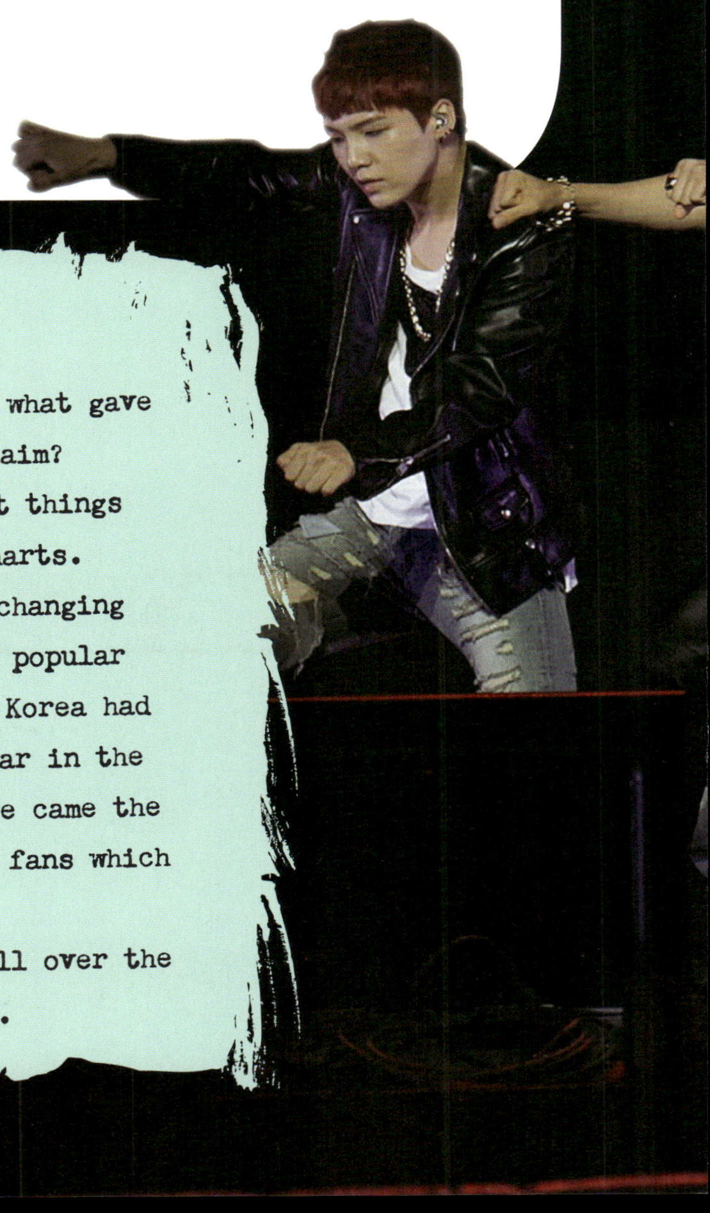

WHY BTS?

Given that hundreds of bands make up the vibrant K-pop scene in South Korea, what gave BTS the edge and propelled it out of its homeland to win worldwide acclaim?

As far back as 2012, Rolling Stone magazine had latched on to the fact that things happening on the South Korean music scene were about to impact the US charts.

As it was, the creation of BTS was perfectly timed. The studio system was changing so that its members weren't the old-fashioned idols who were actually only popular within their own culture. Similarly, the definition of masculinity in South Korea had changed so that boys could experiment with clothes and makeup already popular in the West. Globalisation meant that cultural barriers were falling. Then of course came the impact of social media, which allowed BTS to build up a real connection with fans which undoubtedly helped to grow its fanbase.

Staying true to themselves and performing music which appeals to audiences all over the world, while singing largely in Korean, BTS are truly trailblazing.

TEAMWORK MAKES THE DREAM WORK

While the BTS boys were still at school and could only dream of making it in the music business, the man who was to become their mentor was already making a name for himself in the South Korean music industry.

Bang Si-hyuk was a top music arranger and producer working for one of South Korea's leading music companies when he decided to set up his own studio in 2005. He called his new venture Big Hit Entertainment and set himself the mission of doing things differently, to help his trainees succeed without excessive pressure. He already had the nickname 'Hitman' because of his track record, but even he could scarcely have believed how his new company would thrive.

He was looking for young talents with an edge – and one of his first signings was RM.

The rest of the band was put together by the Big Hit Entertainment audition process. While still focussing on rappers, Suga and J-Hope were the first additional signings, then over the next few years different styles and combinations were tried before the BTS line-up was reorganised and expanded to include four additional new talents; Jin, V, Jimin and Jungkook.

Evidently every one of the boys is a talented singer, dancer, songwriter and performer. However, in common with many South Korean acts, generally the performers will have a speciality and work in subgroups, or 'lines' for the most challenging vocals and dances. With BTS being less staged than other groups, its roles are more blurred, but the usual 'rap line' is RM, Suga and J-Hope, the 'vocal line' is Jungkook, V, Jimin and Jin and the 'dance line' is J-Hope, Jimin and Jungkook. There is also a role called 'visual' relating to good looks, charm and appeal. Again, while this applies to all the BTS band, their official 'visual' is Jin, with V and Jungkook now also getting a lot of attention for their looks, making these three the trio of 'visuals'.

BTS attends the BTS 1st Album "Dark & Wild" ShowCase at the Samsung Card Hall on August 19, 2014 in Seoul, South Korea

Although BTS was set up to incorporate many traditional 'idol' tropes, including looking good with sharp choreography and a strong fusion of hip hop and electronic dance music, there was going to be an important difference. This band was to be real. Instead of perpetuating the 'perfect pop star' idea, the boys wanted to talk about the downsides of life for young people and were not afraid to write about their own flaws and shortcomings.

Bang wanted BTS to be relatable, frank and honest about the pressure of fame. He even imagined that perhaps the band would be able to mentor its fans. The boys of BTS were keen to travel that road. Talented enough to make their own music and lyrics they started to tell stories that their fans wanted – and were ready - to hear.

Their lyrics touch on issues affecting young people today, including mental health, academic stress, bullying and depression. But their songs have lots of positive messages as well, including how young people can find their individuality and overcome complexes and pressures, usually by ' 'loving oneself' – a theme key to much of their work.

In December 2012, six months ahead of their official 'debut', the group, then known as the Bangtan Boys, released a couple of clips on SoundCloud. The boys were seen rapping in English and Korean, and also performing a cover of the Wham classic 'Last Christmas'.

By the time the seven made their official debut in 2013, renamed as BTS, they were completely prepared, preened, and polished with well-rehearsed songs and slick dance routines. The band made its debut on South Korea's M Countdown K-pop chart show, performing No More Dream from their single album 2 Cool 4 Skool.

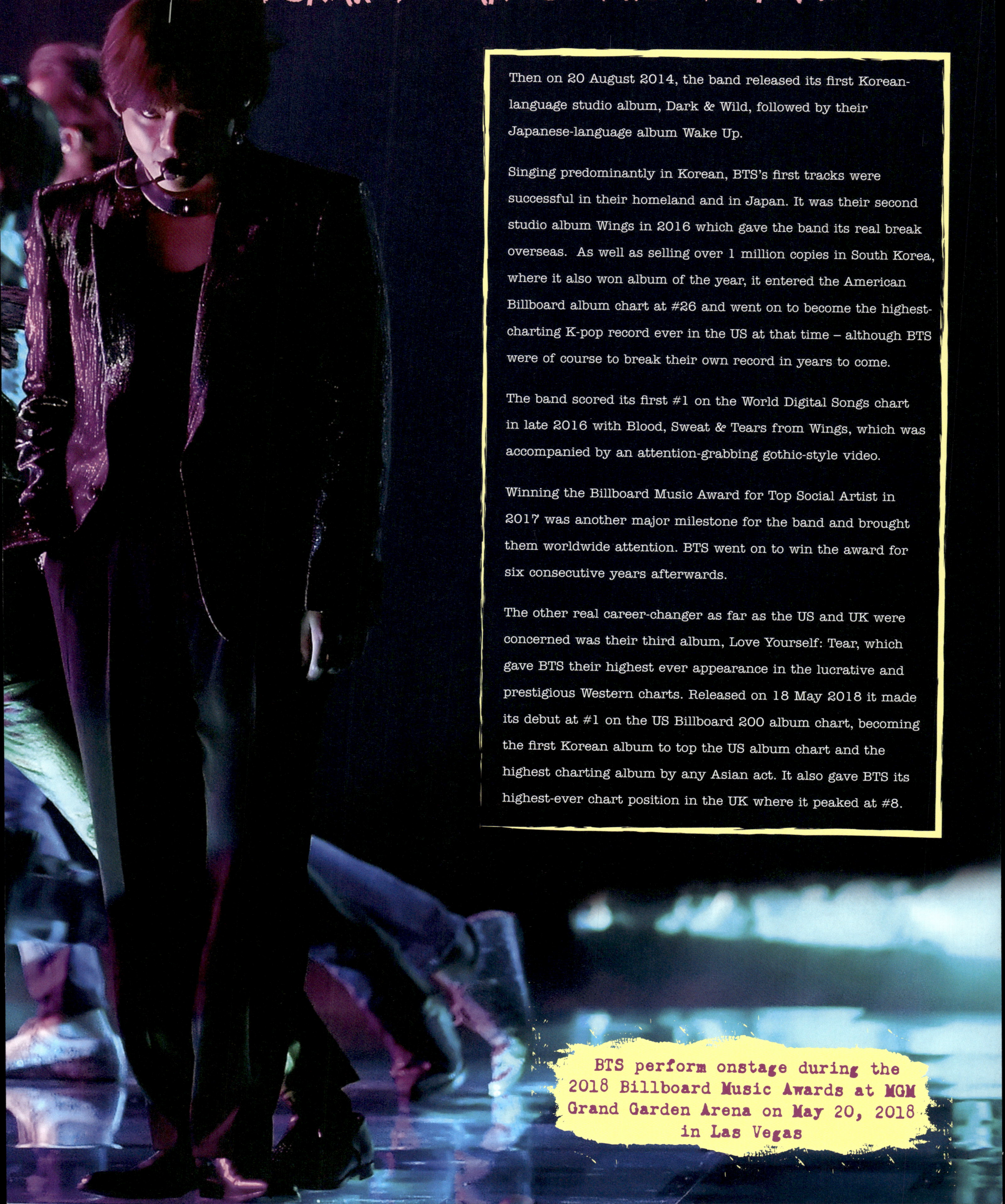

Then on 20 August 2014, the band released its first Korean-language studio album, Dark & Wild, followed by their Japanese-language album Wake Up.

Singing predominantly in Korean, BTS's first tracks were successful in their homeland and in Japan. It was their second studio album Wings in 2016 which gave the band its real break overseas. As well as selling over 1 million copies in South Korea, where it also won album of the year, it entered the American Billboard album chart at #26 and went on to become the highest-charting K-pop record ever in the US at that time – although BTS were of course to break their own record in years to come.

The band scored its first #1 on the World Digital Songs chart in late 2016 with Blood, Sweat & Tears from Wings, which was accompanied by an attention-grabbing gothic-style video.

Winning the Billboard Music Award for Top Social Artist in 2017 was another major milestone for the band and brought them worldwide attention. BTS went on to win the award for six consecutive years afterwards.

The other real career-changer as far as the US and UK were concerned was their third album, Love Yourself: Tear, which gave BTS their highest ever appearance in the lucrative and prestigious Western charts. Released on 18 May 2018 it made its debut at #1 on the US Billboard 200 album chart, becoming the first Korean album to top the US album chart and the highest charting album by any Asian act. It also gave BTS its highest-ever chart position in the UK where it peaked at #8.

BTS perform onstage during the 2018 Billboard Music Awards at MGM Grand Garden Arena on May 20, 2018 in Las Vegas

BTS 2013, Hallyu Dream Concert, October 5, 2013, Gyeongju, South Korea

TEAMWORK MAKES THE DREAM WORK

Once the Western doors were open the hits kept coming, giving BTS the distinction of becoming the fastest-selling group since The Beatles to achieve four #1 albums in less than two years in America.

Next came US #1 albums Love Yourself: Answer (September 2018) Map of The Soul: Persona (April 2019) and then Map of the Soul:7 (March 2020). In the singles charts they did particularly well with their 2019 collaboration featuring Halsey, Boy With Luv which made the top 10 in the US, debuting and peaking at #8 and eventually going platinum. This track also made the top 20 in the UK, reaching #13.

Seven months into 2019, BTS had achieved five #1 hits on Billboard's World Digital Song Sales. Then in August 2020 came the jewel in the crown of the Western charts as BTS became the first Korean act to achieve a #1 on both the Billboard Hot 100 singles chart, the Global 200 and the UK Official Big Top 40 with their mighty hit Dynamite. The catchy, disco-inspired track was the band's first hit to be sung in English. The music video achieved 101 million global views in 24 hours.

BTS were then crowned winners of 2021's IFPI Global Recording Artist of the Year Award. The award is calculated according to an artist's or group's worldwide performance across digital and physical music formats during the year, from streams to vinyl, and covers their entire body of work. The news marked a "landmark moment" for the recording industry, said IFPI, as the South Korean group were the first act to win the award for two consecutive years.

And of course, all the while they were conquering the US and UK, their success in South Korea continued at a historic level. Having sold over 20 million albums on Korea's Gaon Music Chart, BTS became the country's best-selling artist ever, with Map of the Soul:7 the bestselling album ever at the time.

BTS took a further leap into public consciousness, outside of music fans, when Time magazine named BTS on its list of 'Next Generation Leaders'. Two years later the band were named Time magazine's 'Entertainers of the Year'.

04 MAKING MUSIC

BTS is one of the hardest working groups in K-pop producing nine studio albums, four compilations, six EP's and 23 singles in their first eight years together. Alongside that all seven boys have produced solo material. By 2018 BTS had sold more than 10 million albums, setting a record for selling that many records in the shortest time of any Korean act since 2000. They are now the best-selling Korean act of all time.

The band has also released half a dozen Korean and Japanese albums, plus a number of compilation albums, reissues and EPs. Their deft touch means they are as comfortable producing high energy hip hop and electronic dance music as they are with more soulful, confessional-style ballads.

K-pop studios are fond of re-packaging and re-releasing albums so the chronology of the music can appear a little blurred. A good way to look at BTS's output is by 'era' as they describe a particular promotional period of albums and singles connected by a theme, which progresses throughout their career.

BTS onstage at the 2017 American Music Awards at Microsoft Theater on November 19, 2017 in Los Angeles

THE SCHOOL TRILOGY

The first three albums BTS released in Korea are known as the 'School Trilogy' and set up a 'high school bad boy' concept. The first of these albums was 2 Cool 4 Skool, in 2013, from which the band's debut single No More Dream was taken. The lyrics are about pushing back towards a society which says young people can't follow their dreams. We Are Bullet Pt 2 was the other standout single from this album. Then came two mini-albums O!RUL8,2? followed by Skool Luv Affair and its lead single 'Boy in Luv', both released in 2014.

The release of the band's first studio album Dark & Wild marked the end of the 'school' series as the boys transitioned into more mature song themes. Danger and War of Hormone were the standout singles from this album. It made #2 in Korea with sales of 200,000 plus.

THE YOUTH TRILOGY

Next came an image change as BTS emerged to promote their next series of albums, the 'Youth Trilogy', known also as The Most Beautiful Moment in Life (Hwa Yang Yeon Hwa in Korean so sometimes also abbreviated as HYYH). Now their style and sound was less aggressively hip hop; the boys had jettisoned their punky, bad boy look in favour of a more vulnerable and youthful image.

BTS released this HYYH music in three parts during 2015-2016 as The Most Beautiful Moment in Life Parts 1 and 2 EPs, finishing with Young Forever. The theme here was transitioning from youth to young adulthood. While this literally reflected the band members themselves growing up, critics also recognised that it marked the seven musicians moving into a more mature phase and settling into their craft. Hit singles from this period are I Need U, Dope and Run.

I Need U was the track that really changed things for BTS. It was sentimental and really appealing to a young, more mainstream audience. Billboard called it 'one of the greatest K-pop songs of the decade'. It charted at #5 in Korea and gave them their first music show win on SBS MTV's 'The Show'. The Most Beautiful Moment in Life Pt 2 EP was their biggest hit yet, topping the weekly Korean Gaon chart and the Billboard World album chart - the first K-pop track to do so, where it remained for 22 weeks. It also appeared on the regular Billboard album chart, peaking at #171.

WINGS

Then came the era which really cemented the band's success - their second full studio album Wings in October 2016 which took them to the top of the Korean charts, selling 500,000 copies in its first week. Its lead single Blood Sweat and Tears topped eight charts in South Korea and its accompanying video achieved 6 million views on YouTube in 24 hours - the highest ever for a K-pop group at the time.

This was followed by You Never Walk Alone in 2017 which was a repackage with two new singles, Not Today and Spring Day - which many fans consider one of BTS's finest ever recordings.

BTS perform during a Korean cultural event as part of the South Korean President's official visit in France, on October 14, 2018 in Paris

THE LOVE YOURSELF SERIES

This Love Yourself series comprises three albums and a video telling a love story (Love Yourself: Her), moving on to a break-up (Love Yourself: Tear) and finally a realisation that it's necessary to love yourself before you can successfully love somebody else (Love Yourself: Answer).

The release of the Love Yourself: Her album in September 2017 coincided with the band's conquering of the mainstream Western pop charts as BTS at last gained overdue recognition in the West. It spawned one of the band's most memorable and popular singles, the catchy and fun DNA which gave BTS its first entry onto the Billboard Hot 100, coming in at #85 and rising to #67, while its accompanying music video broke the previous record for most viewed K-pop group music video within the first 24 hours with more than 20 million YouTube views.

The follow-up single was Mic Drop (Remix) which made #28 on the Billboard Hot 100, becoming the band's first American top 40 entry as well as the first for any K-pop artist. Both Mic Drop Remix and DNA were to be certified as Gold recordings, with Mic Drop going on to become Platinum making BTS the first Korean act with a Platinum recording.

The second album in the Love Yourself trilogy, Love Yourself: Tear, is a thematic album depicting the end of the 'Her' love affair. Its 11 tracks shift between ballads and emo pop, covering themes of love and loss.

Finally comes Love Yourself: Answer which included the big hit Idol. This track had real resonance for the group as a commentary on the band's disdain for labels and the opinions of others. It's only important that they know and love themselves. This song is also thought to be addressing the stigma attached to idol bands in Asia, similar to the opprobrium heaped upon manufactured boy bands in the west. Again this went to #1 in America.

These three commercially successful albums helped the band begin to gain international recognition. BTS broke YouTube records they had set themselves and collaborated with big Western artists including Nicki Minaj, Desiigner, and Steve Aoki.

V of BTS performs onstage during 102.7 KIIS FM's Jingle Ball 2019, presented by Capital One at the Forum on December 6, 2019 in Los Angeles

MAP OF THE SOUL

2019 saw the start of the Map of the Soul recordings. First was mini-album Map of the Soul: Persona in March 2019 which provided the band with another hit single, the Boy With Luv featuring Halsey track, which gained Platinum sales and record-breaking YouTube views.

It was the best-selling album in South Korean history and gave the band its first #1 in the UK – the first Korean act to achieve this - and in the US, where it was the third album to top the chart in less than 12 months.

Following this would not be easy. But BTS managed it in February 2020 with the release of Map of the Soul:7, the band's fourth studio album. It was especially meaningful for the band because the '7' in the title had several meanings, standing for the seven members of the band, and given the fact that at this point they had been together for seven years, it was partly a memoir of their time together.

Featuring the singles Black Swan and ON, the album sold 4.1 million albums in its first week after release. This launched BTS into legendary status making it the best-selling act in South Korean history and again topping the charts in over 20 countries including the US, the UK, most of Europe, Australia and Canada.

Their fifth studio album Be was created during the strangest of circumstances for the world – the Covid-19 pandemic. Everything came to a halt while the world fought the virus. The boys of BTS, who had expected to spend the year on the road performing on their scheduled world tour, instead found themselves with time on their hands. They

began to write about the effect of quarantine; 'the entire year got stolen' say the lyrics of Fly To My Room, although the main thrust of the album is of course, 'life must go on'.

The track Life Goes On provided BTS with their second US #1 in December 2020, although they had again topped the charts with a remix of Savage Love in collaboration with Jason Derulo and Jawsh in September.

Despite their success in the US and UK album charts, until the summer of 2020 there was still an achievement which had eluded the band – a #1 on the US Billboard Hot 100 and UK Top 40 singles charts. So of course, they had to tick that milestone off too and did it in style with their first English language track, Dynamite, which broke records soon after it was released on 21 August 2020.

DYNAMITE

As well as becoming the top-selling digital song of 2020 in the US with over 1.26 million downloads, Dynamite made #1 in both the US and the UK. Its accompanying retro-style video reached 101 million views on YouTube within the first 24 hours, with more than three million fans tuning in live to watch the clip's premiere.

The upbeat track is heavily influenced by disco music, with lyrics focussing on joy and appreciation for the little things that make life valuable - a message that chimed with the mood of 2020 when the world was in the grip of the Covid-19 pandemic.

BTS said they wanted the song to convey 'positive vibes, energy, hope, love, purity, everything' and were reportedly in tears after hearing the track had topped the Billboard 100 singles chart - making them the first all-Korean pop act to do so.

Dynamite reached 33.9 million US streams in its first week, to debut at #1 on the Billboard Hot 100.

As well as its success in the UK and US, the track made the top 20 in 25 different countries.

Dynamite is one of the few songs not written and produced by band members, but instead co-written by British songwriters David Stewart and Jessica Agombar, who got involved after hearing the band wanted to release an English language track.

Initially a standalone single, the track was later added to the album Be.

05

GOING SOLO

After conquering the world with Dynamite, BTS did something that shocked fans everywhere – they announced they were pressing pause. But this wasn't an ending. As the members explained in their emotional June 2022 dinner video, this was the beginning of "Chapter Two."

BTS coined the phrase 'Chapter Two' to describe what they saw as a turning point in their career.

After nearly a decade defined by their rise to global fame, the band wanted to signal a shift towards a new period of creativity, during which they would prioritise their individual artistry.

In practical terms, 'Chapter Two' became shorthand for an era of solo releases and personal reinvention. Each member pursued distinct musical directions, from introspective singer-songwriter work to harder-edged hip-hop and global pop collaborations, broadening the group's artistic identity even in their absence as a full unit as members fulfilled their mandatory military service, which naturally placed group activities on hold.

Before the hiatus officially began, BTS gave ARMY one last gift: Proof, an anthology album released in June 2022 that celebrated their incredible journey. The three-disc collection featured hit singles, personal favourites, and previously unreleased demos that showed how far they'd come. Lead single Yet to Come (The Most Beautiful Moment) wasn't goodbye – it was a promise that their best work was still ahead.

Then came the bittersweet reality: mandatory military service. All South Korean men must serve approximately 18 months before age 28, and BTS was no exception. Jin led the way in December 2022, followed by J-Hope, then the remaining five members. For nearly four years, ARMY would have to wait for a full group reunion.

But here's where BTS proved they're truly unstoppable. Rather than disappearing, each member used this time to show the world who they were as individual artists. And wow, did they deliver!

The floodgates opened with nine incredible solo albums. RM dropped the artistic masterpiece Indigo, then the experimental Right Place, Wrong Person. J-Hope gave us the bold Jack in the Box and the dance-focused Hope on the Street Vol. 1. Suga's D-Day spawned a massive world tour that grossed over $57 million.

Jin released not one but two albums – Happy and Echo. Jimin made history with Face and MUSE, while Jungkook's Golden proved he's a superstar in any language. V's jazz-influenced Layover showcased his unique baritone voice in ways we'd never heard before.

The achievements were staggering. Jimin's Like Crazy became the first song by a Korean solo artist to hit #1 on the Billboard Hot 100. Jungkook's Seven became a global phenomenon. Each member charted, won awards, and built their own legacies.

From 2022 onwards, during and between their military hiatus, the members' solo careers really took off, with each member taking to stages around the world on their own.

BTS attend the 61st Annual Grammy Awards at Staples Center on February 10, 2019 in Los Angeles, California

J-HOPE

HOPE ON THE STREET TOUR (2025)

Asia and North America tour
Headlined Lollapalooza (Chicago, 2022) – first Korean solo artist
Headlined Lollapalooza Berlin (July 2025)

SUGA

D-DAY WORLD TOUR (2023)

26 concerts across Asia and North America
318,000+ attendees
Grossed 57.1 million
Highest-grossing Asian solo tour of 2023

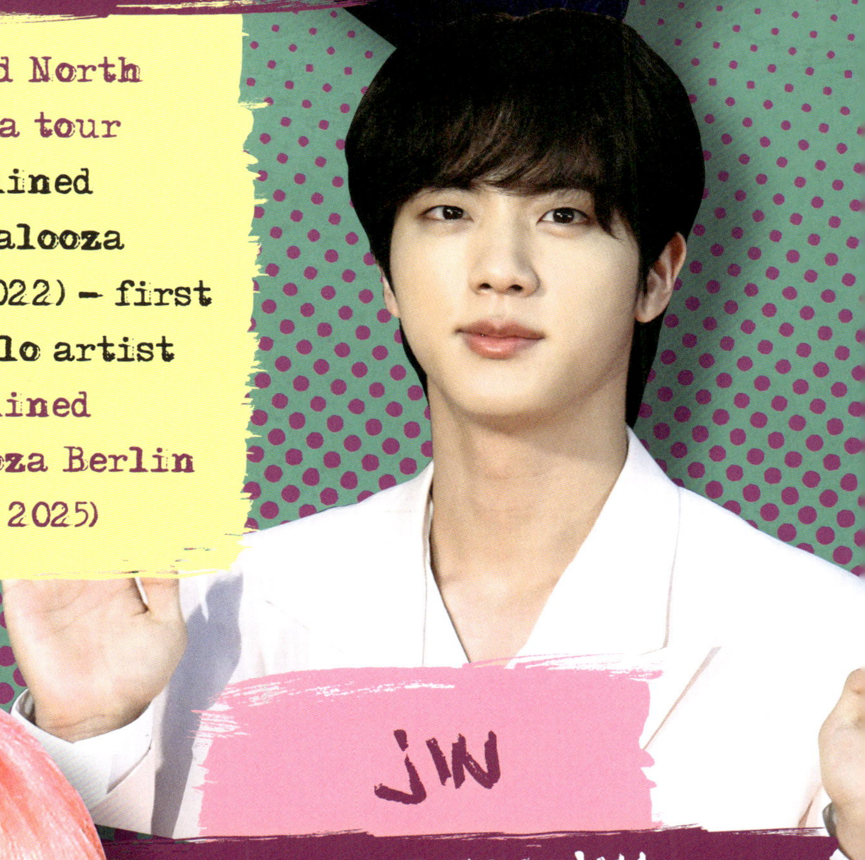

JIN

RUN SEOKJIN (2024-2025)

Special fan meetings and showcases
Performances for Happy and Echo albums

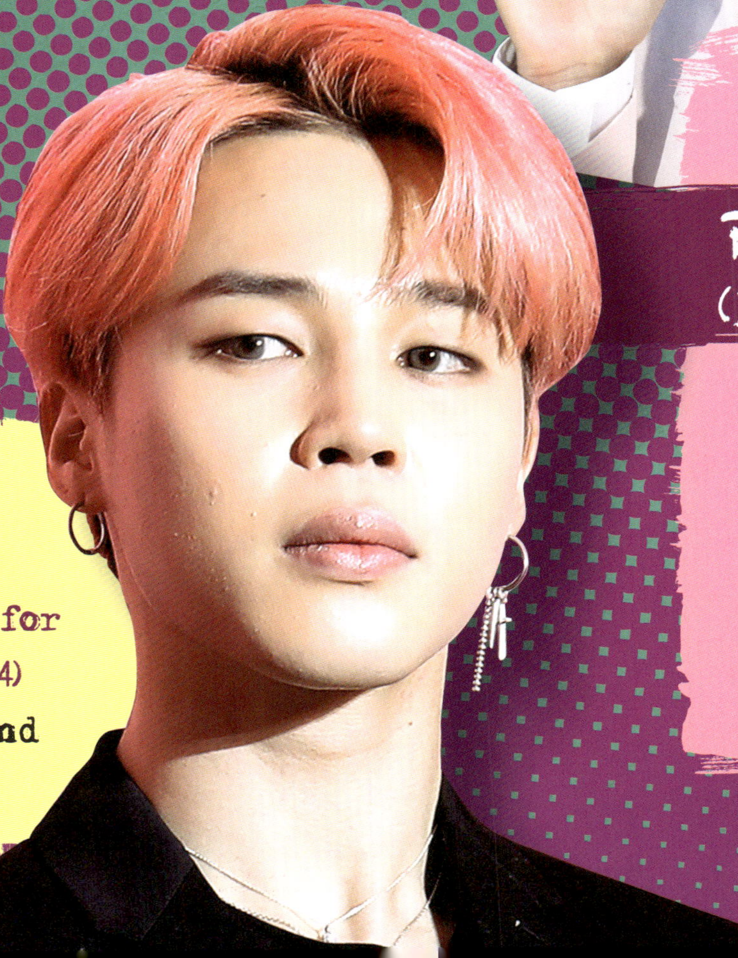

JIMIN

Promotional performances for Face (2023) and MUSE (2024)
Television appearances and special showcases

RM

Showcase events for Indigo (2022)
and Right Place, Wrong Person (2024)
Festival and television appearances

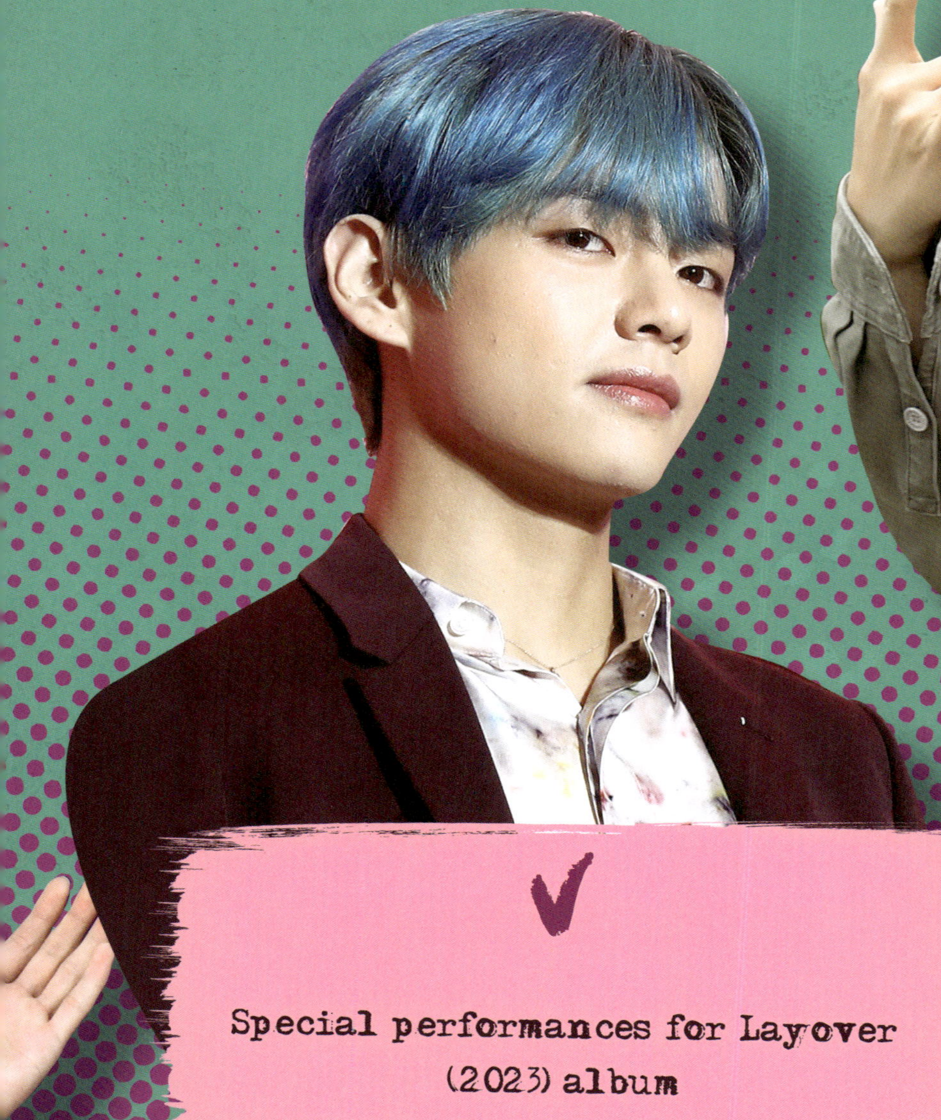

V

Special performances for Layover (2023) album

JUNGKOOK

Promotional performances for Golden (2023) album
FIFA World Cup Opening Ceremony (Qatar, 2022)
Major US television appearances

08

BTS ARMY MARCHES ON

BTS fans are quite simply like no others. An incredible organisation, self-styled as ARMY, which stands for 'Adorable Representative MCs for Youth' they've been described by US magazine Vulture as 'the most quantifiable active fandom in history'.

ARMY comprises tens of millions of devoted followers, who are particularly active on social media. They come from all over the world and support each other and the band unreservedly. 'Even if there is a language barrier, once the music starts, people react pretty much the same wherever we go,' says Suga. 'It feels like the music really brings us together.'

What is particularly notable about ARMY is its loyalty and organisational ability to mobilise to support BTS during every album, song and video release.

They use message boards, group chats and podcasts to analyse the meanings in the band's lyrics and videos, searching for messages, metaphors and cultural references. They also share stories about how BTS's music and lyrics have saved them from dark situations and helped them cope with difficulties in their lives.

BTS regularly speak of their incredible connection with ARMY, describing their fans as; 'the most passionate, the best and our motivation. They mean a lot to us. People speaking all different languages and coming from different countries, different ethnicities. It's an honour that they all listen to and enjoy our songs. It's what drives us to perform'.

The BTS ARMY pose with photos of their idols outside the 2017 American Music Awards, November 19, 2017 at the Microsoft Theater at LA Live, in Los Angeles

07

ARIRANG MARKS A TRIUMPHANT RETURN

ARIRANG MARKS A TRIUMPHANT RETURN

Once all the BTS boys had completed their military service, the band reunited in 2025 to begin their most anticipated chapter yet.

The release of their comeback studio album ARIRANG in March 2026 marked a seismic return for BTS and quickly reaffirmed their global dominance.

Within 24 hours the album sold an extraordinary 3.98 million copies – driven largely by physical album sales - the biggest first-day total of their career and one of the largest ever recorded. In South Korea alone, it went on to sell 4.2 million copies in its first week.

Internationally, ARIRANG delivered equally striking results. It debuted at #1 on the US Billboard 200 with 641,000 album-equivalent units, including over half a million pure sales, marking the group's seventh US chart-topper and the biggest week for any group since modern chart metrics were introduced. The album also topped charts across major markets including the UK, Germany and Australia.

Streaming figures were similarly impressive. All 14 tracks from the album simultaneously occupied the top 14 positions on Spotify's global chart, contributing to more than 110 million streams on the platform in a single day. The album also set a new first-day streaming record for a pop group on Apple Music.

Critically, ARIRANG was praised for its scale and ambition and its polished, globally oriented sound. It marked a comeback that combines commercial firepower with cultural weight, re-establishing BTS at the centre of global pop.

To give the band the last word, the members say they would like to be remembered as; 'Seven boys who are sincere in their craft, in their lyrics, and in their actions' – and their 2025 reunion proves they're nowhere near finished.

RM and V react after being discharged from their mandatory military service on June 10, 2025

J-HOPE headlining Lollapalooza, Berlin, 2025

RM

Favourite Brands: Yohji, Y-3, WTAPS, Neighbourhood, Visvim

BTS onstage for the 2020 American Music Awards on November 22, 2020 in South Korea

SUGA
Favourite Brands: Mastermind Japan, Visvim, Gucci, Balenciaga, Saint Laurent

BTS perform 'DNA' onstage during the 2017 American Music Awards held at Microsoft Theater on November 19, 2017 in Los Angeles

j-HOPE

Favourite Brands: Raf Simons, YEEZY, Louis Vuitton, JW Anderson, Off-White

2017 American Music Awards rehearsals at Microsoft Theater, November 17, 2017, Los Angeles

JIN
Favourite Brands: Balenciaga, Gucci, Givenchy, Raf Simons, Visvim, Off - White

BTS perform onstage at the 2018 Billboard Music Awards at MGM Grand Garden Arena on May 20, 2018 in Las Vegas

JIMIN

Favourite Brands: Raf Simons, Gucci, Prada, JW Anderson, Thom Browne, Balenciaga

2017 American Music Awards rehearsals at Microsoft Theater on November 17, 2017 in Los Angeles

V

Favourite Brands: Gucci, Louis Vuitton, Hermès, Burberry

Press conference marking the release of its new album "Map of the Soul Persona" at Dongdaemun Design Plaza in central Seoul on April 17, 2019 in Seoul, South Korea

JUNGKOOK

Favourite Brands: Gucci, WTAPS, Calvin Klein, Raf Simons, Monitaly

BTS perform during a Korean cultural event as part of South Korean president official visit in France, on October 14, 2018 in Paris

BTS attends the 61st Annual GRAMMY Awards at Staples Center on February 10, 2019 in Los Angeles, California

BTS perform onstage during the 2018 Billboard Music Awards at MGM Grand Garden Arena on May 20, 2018 in Las Vegas